ABC'S OF WHO I AM
DECREEING WHO GOD SAYS I AM
BY LUCIA M. CLABORN
COPYRIGHT (C) 2020 BY LUCIA M. CLABORN –
ALL RIGHTS RESERVED. SECOND PRINTING.
PUBLISHED IN THE UNITED STATES OF AMERICA
BY LUCIA M. CLABORN – 2586 COUNTY ROAD 165,
MOULTON, AL 35650 WWW.LUCIACLABORN.COM

COVER ARTWORK BY DONNA L. AMMONS – A BRUSH WITH JESUS STUDIO
WWW.ABRUSHWITHJESUS.COM

THE HOLY BIBLE, BEREAN STUDY BIBLE, BSB COPYRIGHT (C) 2016, 2018 BY BIBLE HUB USED BY PERMISSION.
ALL RIGHTS RESERVED WORLDWIDE.

NEW AMERICAN STANDARD BIBLE, (NASB) COPYRIGHT (C) 1960, 1962, 1963, 1968, 1971, 1972, 1973,
1975, 1977, 1995 BY THE LOCKMAN FOUNDATION USED BY PERMISSION. WWW.LOCKMAN.ORG

SCRIPTURE QUOTATIONS ARE FROM THE ESV BIBLE (THE HOLY BIBLE, ENGLISH STANDARD VERSION),
COPYRIGHT (C) 2001 BY CROSSWAY BIBLES,
A PUBLISHING MINISTRY OF GOOD NEWS PUBLISHERS. USED BY PERMISSION. ALL RIGHTS RESERVED.

SCRIPTURE QUOTATIONS TAKEN FROM THE AMPLIFIED BIBLE (AMPC), COPYRIGHT (C) 1954, 1958, 1962, 1964,
1965, 1987 BY THE LOCKMAN FOUNDATION,
USED BY PERMISSION. WWW.LOCKMAN.ORG

THE MESSAGE IS QUOTED. "SCRIPTURE TAKEN FROM THE MESSAGE. COPYRIGHT (C) 1993, 1994, 1995, 1996,
2000, 2001, 2002.
USED BY PERMISSION OF NAVPRESS PUBLISHING GROUP.

DEDICTION

THIS BOOK IS LOVINGLY DEDICATED TO MY CHILDREN

- DANIEL, MCKENZIE, EMILY & KATIE -

YOU HAVE A MUCH GREATER UNDERSTANDING OF
WHO YOU ARE IN JESUS CHRIST
AND ARE AWESOME EXAMPLES OF THE POWER
OF DECREEING GOD'S WORD IN YOUR LIFE.

YOU ARE THE TREASURES OF MY HEART AND
I THANK GOD FOR YOU!

MUCH LOVE,

MOTHER

ACKNOWLEDGEMENTS

I WOULD LIKE TO THANK
DONNA AMMONS
FOR BEING MY GREATEST CHEERLEADER.

LINDA STARKS
FOR BEING MY PRAYER WARRIOR AND INTERCESSOR.

AND

TANYA TENICA PAXOT
FOR BEING MY BUSINESS MIDWIFE TO ACTIVATE AND
INSPIRING ME TO ACCOMPLISH MY DREAMS.

YOU LADIES ARE PRICELESS TO ME AND I APPRECIATE AND
VALUE OUR FRIENDSHIP.

A

I DECREE I AM

The Apple of God's Eye DEUTERONOMY 32:10
Abundantly Provided For EPHESIANS 3:20
Abounding In Faith COLOSSIANS 2:7
As He is in This World 1 JOHN 4:17
Accepted in the Beloved EPHESIANS 1:6
Anointed 1 JOHN 2:27
Approved 2 CORINTHIANS 5:21
Abiding in Him 1 JOHN 3:24
Anxious for Nothing PHILIPPIANS 4:6
Living the Abundant Life JOHN 10:10
Above Only and Not Beneath DEUTERONOMY 28:13
Amazing PSALM 118:23
Using My Authority LUKE 10:19
Receiving All Things 2 PETER 1:3
Acquitted 1 JOHN 1:9

B

I DECREE I AM

Baptized With Holy Spirit ACTS 2:38
The Bride of Christ 2 CORINTHIANS 11:2
A Believer JOHN 6:47
Buried with Christ ROMANS 6:4
Blood Bought I CORINTHIANS 6:20
Born Again of Incorruptible Seed I PETER 1:23
Born of God I JOHN 4:7
Being Conformed to His Image ROMANS 8:29
Full of Boldness HEBREWS 10:19
Believing HEBREWS 10:39
Blessed GALATIANS 3:9
The Beloved ROMANS 1:7

I DECREE I HAVE

Boldness in the Day of Judgement I JOHN 4:17

C

I DECREE I AM

A Child of the Promise ROMANS 9:8
Confident PHILIPPIANS 1:6
Chosen EPHESIANS 1:4
Called ROMANS 8:30
A Child of God ROMANS 8:17
Crucified with Christ GALATIANS 2:20
Complete in Him COLOSSIANS 2:10
A Citizen of Heaven PHILIPPIANS 3:20
Clothed with Righteousness EPHESIANS 6:14
Created In God's Image EPHESIANS 4:24
A Conqueror I CORINTHIANS 15:7
Cleansed from All Sin I JOHN 1:7
Calling Those Things Which Are Not as Though They Are ROMANS 4:17

D

I DECREE I AM

Delivered from Darkness COLOSSIANS 1:3
Dead to the Law ROMANS 7:4
Delivered from the Dominion of Sin ROMANS 6:14
Dressed in God's Armor EPHESIANS 6:11
Disciplined I CORINTHIANS 9:27
Delivered from the Evils of This World GALATIANS 1:4
A Do-er of the Word JOHN 14:12
Dead to Sin ROMANS 6:2
Walking in Dominion GENESIS 1:26
A Disciple of Jesus Christ JOHN 12:35
Not Giving Place to the Devil EPHESIANS 4:27

I DECREE I AM

Established in the Faith COLOSSIANS 2:7
Energetic ROMANS 12:8
Enriched in the Faith I CORINTHIANS 1:5
Empowered EPHESIANS 6:10
Equipped 2 TIMOTHY 3:17
Elected of God COLOSSIANS 3:12
Excellent TITUS 3:8
Enthusiastic ROMANS 12:8
Established to the End I CORINTHIANS 1:8

I DECREE I HAVE

Everlasting Life JOHN 5:24
All Enemies Defeated DEUTERONOMY 28:7
Everlasting Release HEBREWS 9:12
Eternal Life JOHN 17:3

I DECREE I AM

Financially Blessed 2 CORINTHIANS 8:9
A Fellow Heir with Jesus EPHESIANS 6:6
Full of Faith HEBREWS 10:22
Forgiven COLOSSIANS 2:13
Free HEBREWS 2:15, JOHN 8:36
A Faithful Follower of Jesus REVELATIONS 17:14
Forgiven of All Unrighteousness 1 JOHN 1:9
Filled with Holy Spirit ACTS 2:4
Full of Understanding PSALM 49:3
Free from Condemnation ROMANS 8:1
Walking in the Favor of God and Man LUKE 2:52
Using Overcoming Faith 1 JOHN 5:4-5
Free from Fear 2 TIMOTHY 1:7

G

I DECREE I AM

Guaranteed an Inheritance EPHESIANS 1:11

God's Child ROMANS 8:16

Gifted ROMANS 12:6

Full of God 1 JOHN 4:4

Graced 2 CORINTHIANS 9:8

God's Workmanship EPHESIANS 2:10

Wearing the Garment of Praise ISAIAH 61:3

Receiving All God's Promises 2 PETER 1:4

Glorifying God With My Mouth and Words
ROMANS 15:6

Greater Because God in Me is Greater 1 JOHN 4:4

I DECREE I HAVE

Been Given the Measure of Faith ROMANS 12:3

I DECREE I AM

Helped ROMANS 10:13

Holy EPHESIANS 1:4

An Heir TITUS 3:7

Healed by the Stripes on Jesus Body I PETER 2:24

The Head and Not the Tail DEUTERONOMY 28:13

Happy PHILIPPIANS 1:8

Hid with Christ COLOSSIANS 3:3

I DECREE I HAVE

All the Holy Spirit is: Comfort, Spirit of Truth, Teacher, Glories Jesus, Remembrance, Testimony of Jesus, a Witness of Jesus JOHN 14:16

The Heathen for my Inheritance PSALM 2:8

I

I DECREE I AM

In this World but Not of It JOHN 15:19
In Christ by His Doing EPHESIANS 1:10
Indwelled by Holy Spirit TITUS 3:7
Instructed TITUS 2:12
In Christ COLOSSIANS 3:3
An Instrument of the Righteousness of God ROMANS 6:13
Not Inferior 2 CORINTHIANS 11:5
In the Spirit ROMANS 8:9

I DECREE I HAVE

Jesus as my Intercessor ROMANS 8:34
An Inheritance EPHESIANS 1:11

J

I DECREE I AM

Justified TITUS 3:7
Justified by Faith ROMANS 3:28
Full of Great Joy JOHN 16:24
Justified by God ROMANS 8:33
Full of Joy JOHN 17:13
Loving Jesus with my Whole Heart ROMANS 10:9
Justified by the Blood of Jesus ROMANS 5:9

I DECREE I HAVE

Jesus as My Lord ROMANS 10:10

K

I DECREE I AM

In the Kingdom of God MATTHEW 6:33

Kept From the Evil One 2 THESSALONIANS 3:3

A Keeper of His Word 1 JOHN 2:5

Full of Kindness GALATIANS 5:22

One of a Kingdom of Priests REVELATIONS 5:10

Knowing I Have Eternal Life 1 JOHN 5:12

A Keeper of His Testimonies PSALM 119:146

Knowing All Things Work Together for My Good

ROMANS 8:28

Knowing the Mystery of God's Will EPHESIANS 1:9

L

I DECREE I AM

A Lender DEUTERONOMY 28:12

Not Lacking JAMES 1:4

A Landowner JOSHUA 1:3

Full of Life 1 JOHN 5:12

Putting On Love COLOSSIANS 3:14

Lead by Holy Spirit ROMANS 8:14

The Light of the World EPHESIANS 5:8

The Lord's ROMANS 14:8

Living JOHN 11:25

In the Likeness of His Resurrection ROMANS 6:5

Loved 1 JOHN 4:10

Walking in Liberty 2 CORINTHIANS 3:17

M

I DECREE I AM

Made Alive COLOSSIANS 2:13

A Member of the Body of Christ I CORINTHIANS 12:12

Exercising Mountain Moving Faith MARK 11:25

A Minister of Reconciliation 2 CORINTHIANS 5:18

Mighty in Words and in Deeds ACTS 7:22

Made Near to God by the Blood of Jesus EPHESIANS 2:13

Renewing my Mind ROMANS 12:1

More Than a Conqueror ROMANS 8:37

Motivated PHILIPPIANS 2:3

Using My Measure of Faith ROMANS 12:3

Made in the Image of God I CORINTHIANS 11:7

Married to Jesus ROMANS 7:4

Setting My Mind on the Things of God COLOSSIANS 3:2

The Mind of Christ I CORINTHIANS 2:16

I DECREE I AM

A New Creature, a New Creation 2 CORINTHIANS 5:17

Not Beneath DEUTERONOMY 28:13

Walking in Newness of Life ROMANS 6:4

Not Conformed to This World ROMANS 12:2

Asking Everything in the Name of Jesus JOHN 14:14

Not a Slave of Sin ROMANS 6:6

Not a Borrower DEUTERONOMY 28:12

Never Under Condemnation JOHN 3:18

Not Lacking Anything PHILIPPIANS 4:19

Never Put to Shame ROMANS 9:33

Not Living According to the Flesh but According to the Spirit ROMANS 8:4

O

I DECREE I AM

Overtaken With Blessings DEUTERONOMY 28:12

A Sweet Smelling Odor PHILIPPIANS 4:18

Not Offended 1 CORINTHIANS 8:13

One in Christ ROMANS 12:5

An Orator of God's Word ACTS 24:1

Obeying Wholeheartedly ROMANS 6:17

An Owner LUKE 19:33

Abraham's Offspring GALATIANS 3:29

An Overcomer REVELATIONS 12:11

A Child of Obedience 1 PETER 1:2

I DECREE I AM

A Partaker of the Divine Nature 2 PETER 1:4

The Possessor of All Things 2 PETER 1:3

Patient ROMANS 12:12

Receiving the Promise ACTS 2:2, 2 PETER 1:4

A Pray-er JAMES 5:16

Full of Peace PHILIPPIANS 4:6

Prosperous 3 JOHN 2

A Praiser HEBREWS 13:15

Purchased by the Blood of Jesus 1 PETER 1:19

A Peculiar Person 1 PETER 2:9

Protected PSALM 138:8

Full of Power MARK 16:17, LUKE 10:19

Prepared 2 Corinthians 5:5

Pressing Toward the Goal Philippians 3:13

I DECREE I AM

Quickened Together with Christ EPHESIANS 2:5

Quickened Together with Him COLOSSIANS 2:13

Quickened in my Mortal Body by the Same Spirit that Raised Jesus from the Dead ROMANS 8:11

Quiet ACTS 22:2

Not a Quitter I CORINTHIANS 16:13

Qualified to be a Partaker of God's Inheritance COLOSSIANS 1:12

Working in Quietness and Eating my Own Bread I THESSALONIANS 3:12

I DECREE I AM

Raised from the Dead COLOSSIANS 2:12

Redeemed 1 CORINTHIANS 1:30

Rooted in Christ COLOSSIANS 2:7

Righteous 2 CORINTHIANS 5:21

Rooted in Love EPHESIANS 3:17

Rejoicing ROMANS 5:2

Receiving All God's Promises 2 CORINTHIANS 1:20, 2 PETER 1:4

Reconciled to God EPHESIANS 2:16

Royalty 1 PETER 2:9

Resting HEBREWS 4:3

Ruling and Reigning in Love ROMANS 5:17

Rich 2 CORINTHIANS 8:9

Refreshed ACTS 3:19

Radiant PSALM 34:5

I DECREE I AM

Saved by Jesus' Death and Life ROMANS 5:10
Standing Firm PHILIPPIANS 2:27
Set Free JOHN 8:36
Strong in the Lord EPHESIANS 6:10
Soul Prospering 3 JOHN 2
Saved from God's Wrath ROMANS 5:9
Sanctified by Truth JOHN 17:17
Set Apart JEREMIAH 1:5
Seated in Heavenly Places EPHESIANS 2:6
Spiritually Blessed EPHESIANS 1:3
Set in the Body of Christ 1 CORINTHIANS 12:18
A Servant of Righteousness ROMANS 6:18
The Salt of the Earth MATTHEW 5:13
Secure PSALM 37:28
Self-controlled 1 CORINTHIANS 9:25
Speaking the Truth in Love EPHESIANS 4:15

T

I DECREE I AM

Translated into God's Kingdom COLOSSIANS 1:13
Tenderhearted EPHESIANS 4:32
Thankful to God 2 CORINTHIANS 2:14
A Good Tree MATTHEW 7:17
Teaching the Word in Holy Spirit's Power MATTHEW 28:20
A Tither HEBREWS 7:5
Not the Tail DEUTERONOMY 28:13
A Testimony unto God 2 THESSALONIANS 1:10
Not Tempted JAMES 1:13
Full of God's Treasure DEUTERONOMY 28:12
Always Triumphant in Christ Jesus 2 CORINTHIANS 2:14
Thinking Right Thoughts PHILIPPIANS 4:8
Speaking With a Tongue of the Learned ISAIAH 50:4
A Temple of Holy Spirit 1 CORINTHIANS 3:16

U

I DECREE I AM

Not One With an Unbelieving Heart HEBREWS 3:12

Used by God I CORINTHIANS 12:11

Untouched by the Devil I JOHN 5:18

Un-tied From All Curses GALATIANS 3:13

In the Unity of the Faith EPHESIANS 4:3

Under a Better Covenant HEBREWS 8:6

Maintaining the Unity of the Spirit EPHESIANS 4:3

Not Unequally Yoked 2 CORINTHIANS 6:14

Under Grace ROMANS 6:14

United Together in the Likeness of Jesus ROMANS 6:5

Led by an Unction From the Holy One I JOHN 2:20

Understanding All Things I JOHN 5:20

V

I DECREE I AM

A Victorious Child of God I CORINTHIANS 15:57

Valued EPHESIANS 2:4-5

Very Obedient to the Voice of Holy Spirit I CORINTHIANS 12:7

Virtuous PROVERBS 31:10

Vigilant I PETER 5:8

A Listener to the Voice of the Good Shepherd JOHN 10:4

Victorious Over the World I JOHN 5:4

Receiving God's Visions ACTS 2:17

Valiant PSALM 60:12

I DECREE I AM

Wealthy DEUTERONOMY 8:18
God's Workmanship EPHESIANS 2:10
A Lover of the Word of God COLOSSIANS 3:16
A Witness of Jesus Christ JOHN 15:27
Full of the Life-giving Word of God HEBREWS 4:12
Washed in the Blood of Jesus REVELATIONS 1:5
Full of Wisdom JAMES 1:5
Walking in Faith 2 CORINTHIANS 5:7
Full of Witty Inventions PROVERBS 8:12
Using My Supernatural Weapons of Warfare
2 CORINTHIANS 10:3
A Warrior PSALM 144:5
Wonderfully and Fearfully Made PSALM 139:14
Without Blame EPHESIANS 1:4
A Worshipper I PHILIPPIANS 3:3
A Doer of Whatever is True and Just PHILIPPIANS 4:8
Well Able 2 TIMOTHY 1:12

X

I DECREE I AM

A Beneficiary of the Exceeding Great and Precious Promises of God 2 PETER 1:4

In the Covenant of Knowing God is able to do Exceedingly Above and Beyond All That I Could Ask or Imagine EPHESIANS 3:20

Excelling in Building Up the Church 1 CORINTHIANS 14:12

Listening to Excellent Things PROVERBS 8:6

Y

I DECREE I AM

Taught From My Youth PSALM 71:17
Yielding to Obedience ROMANS 6:16
A Yokefellow With Jesus PHILIPPIANS 4:3
Living With My Youth Restored ISAIAH 40:31
Having My Youthful Strength Restored as the Eagles PSALM 103:5
Yoked to Jesus MATTHEW 11:28
Not Yielding to Unrighteousness ROMANS 6:13

Z

I DECREE I AM

Zealous for Good Works TITUS 2:14

Zion - God's Dwelling Place PSALM 133:3

Zealous to Serve God TITUS 2:14

Full of Zeal for God 2 CORINTHIANS 7:11

Zealous for Spiritual Gifts 1 CORINTHIANS 14:12

Zoe - Full of Life JOHN 10:10

Zealously Sought After GALATIANS 4:17

Zealous and Repent REVELATIONS 3:19

Zealous to Love My Neighbor as Myself TITUS 2:14

P

PRAYER OF SALVATION

HEAVENLY FATHER, I COME TO YOU IN THE NAME OF JESUS. YOUR WORD SAYS, "AND WHOEVER CALLS OUT FOR HELP TO ME, GOD, WILL BE SAVED." ACTS 2:21 (THE MESSAGE BIBLE). I'M CALLING ON YOU NOW. I PRAY AND ASK JESUS TO COME INTO MY HEART, BE LORD OVER MY LIFE ACCORDING TO ROMANS 10:9-10 (THE PASSION TRANSLATION BIBLE) "AND WHAT IS GOD'S "LIVING MESSAGE"? IT IS THE REVELATION OF FAITH FOR SALVATION, WHICH IS THE MESSAGE THAT WE PREACH. FOR IF YOU PUBLICLY DECLARE WITH YOUR MOUTH THAT JESUS IS LORD AND BELIEVE IN YOUR HEART THAT GOD RAISED HIM FROM THE DEAD, YOU WILL EXPERIENCE SALVATION. THE HEART THAT BELIEVES IN HIM RECEIVES THE GIFT OF THE RIGHTEOUSNESS OF GOD—AND THEN THE MOUTH GIVES THANKS TO SALVATION." I DO THAT NOW. I BELIEVE IN MY HEART THAT GOD RAISED HIM FROM THE DEAD AND I CONFESS JESUS IS LORD.

I AM NOW BORN AGAIN! I AM A CHRISTIAN - ALMIGHTY GOD'S CHOSEN CHILD!

YOUR WORD ALSO SAYS, "AS BAD AS YOU ARE, YOU WOULDN'T THINK OF SUCH A THING, YOU'RE AT LEAST DECENT TO YOUR OWN CHILDREN. AND DON'T YOU THINK THE FATHER WHO CONCEIVED YOU IN LOVE WILL GIVE THE HOLY SPIRIT WHEN YOU ASK HIM?" LUKE 11:13 (THE MESSAGE BIBLE) I'M ASKING YOU TO FILL ME WITH THE HOLY SPIRIT. HOLY SPIRIT, RISE UP WITHIN ME AS I PRAISE GOD. I EXPECT TO SPEAK WITH OTHER TONGUES AS YOU GIVE ME UTTERANCE. "THEN, LIKE A WILDFIRE, THE HOLY SPIRIT SPREAD THROUGH THEIR RANKS, AND THEY STARTED SPEAKING IN A NUMBER OF DIFFERENT LANGUAGES AS THE SPIRIT PROMPTED THEM." ACTS 2:4 (THE MESSAGE BIBLE).

NOW, WORSHIP AND PRAISE GOD AS YOU ARE FILLED WITH THE HOLY SPIRIT AND SPEAK IN YOUR HEAVENLY LANGUAGE, OR OTHER TONGUES.

ABOUT LUCIA CLABORN

LIKE MOST PEOPLE LUCIA CLABORN HAS ENCOUNTERED MANY CHALLENGES IN HER LIFE; HOWEVER, SHE'S LEARNED TO RELY ON THE POWER AND AUTHORITY OF JESUS CHRIST, MAKING THE BIBLE HER FINAL AUTHORITY IN LIFE. SHE KNOWS GOD IS MORE THAN ENOUGH TO MEET HER EVERY NEED; AND JESUS IS THE SAME YESTERDAY, TODAY, AND TOMORROW.

SHE'S FIRMLY ROOTED IN THE FACT THAT JESUS CAME TO BRING LIFE AND LIFE MORE ABUNDANTLY. SHE BELIEVES THE SPOKEN WORD HAS POWER, AND THAT GOD GIVES HIS CHILDREN AUTHORITY TO WALK IN DOMINION, AND RULE AND REIGN IN THEIR WORLD. HER HEARTBEAT IS TO TEACH PEOPLE TO STAND ON THE WORD OF GOD, DECREE AND DECLARE THEIR DESIRED WORLD INTO EXISTENCE, AND RELEASE THEIR FAITH TO RECEIVE THEIR HEART'S DESIRES. SHE ENCOURAGES OTHERS TO LIVE THE VICTORIOUS LIFE BY CHANGING THEIR NEGATIVE THOUGHTS AND WORDS OF DEFEAT INTO POSITIVE, FAITH-FILLED DECLARATIONS. WHATEVER MOUNTAIN IS IN YOUR LIFE, YOU CAN OVERCOME IT BY THE BLOOD OF THE LAMB AND THE WORD OF YOUR TESTIMONY.

LUCIA'S BEEN WRITING FOR MORE THAN 30 YEARS, AND HAS BEEN PUBLISHED IN NUMEROUS NEWSPAPERS, MAGAZINES AND PERIODICALS. SHE'S MARRIED TO DANNY AND THEY HAVE FOUR GROWN CHILDREN, DANIEL (MAGEN), MCKENZIE (JAKE), EMILY (TYLER) AND KATIE; TWO GRANDCHILDREN, BRANTLEY AND JACKSON; AND THEY MAKE THEIR HOME IN ALABAMA.

ABOUT THIS BOOK

IF YOU WANT TO CHANGE YOUR WORLD, CHANGE WHAT YOU ARE SPEAKING! THE "I AM" FAITH DECLARATIONS IN THIS BOOK WILL GIVE YOU A BETTER UNDERSTANDING OF WHO GOD MADE YOU TO BE IN JESUS CHRIST! THEY WILL BUILD YOUR CONFIDENCE TO WALK IN A GREATER LEVEL OF VICTORY IN YOUR LIFE WHEN YOU DECREE THEM IN FAITH. YOU WILL SEE YOURSELF THROUGH GOD'S EYES, JUST AS HE SEES YOU IN HIS WORD.

THESE ARE PROMISES OF WHO GOD SAYS YOU ARE AS A BORN-AGAIN CHILD OF GOD. WHEN YOU DECLARE GOD'S PROMISES FROM HIS WORD OVER YOURSELF AND YOUR FAMILY, YOU CANNOT FAIL TO PRODUCE A HARVEST AND BRING FORTH THE RICHNESS AND FULLNESS OF ETERNAL LIFE INTO YOUR LIFE WHILE YOU ARE HERE ON THE EARTH. GOD'S WORD NOT ONLY DESCRIBES A GLORIOUS FUTURE, IT IS GOD'S APPOINTED MEANS TO CREATE THE FUTURE YOU WANT FOR YOU AND YOUR FAMILY!

AS YOU DECREE GOD'S WORD OVER YOUR LIFE AND YOUR FAMILY, IT WILL NOT RETURN TO YOU EMPTY HANDED. IT WILL PRODUCE A GREAT HARVEST ACCORDING TO ISAIAH 55:10-11 WHICH TELLS YOU, "FOR AS THE RAIN AND THE SNOW COME DOWN FROM HEAVEN AND DO NOT RETURN THERE BUT WATER THE EARTH, MAKING IT BRING FORTH AND SPROUT, GIVING SEED TO THE SOWER AND BREAD TO THE EATER, SO SHALL MY WORD BE THAT GOES OUT FROM MY MOUTH; IT SHALL NOT RETURN TO ME EMPTY, BUT IT SHALL ACCOMPLISH THAT WHICH I PURPOSE, AND SHALL SUCCEED IN THE THING FOR WHICH I SENT IT." ESV

www.ingramcontent.com/pod-product-compliance
Lightning Source LLC
Chambersburg PA
CBHW040108120526
44589CB00039B/2799